Kansas City Chiefs
Trivia Quiz Book

500 Questions on All Things Red and Gold

Chris Bradshaw

Front cover image created by headfuzz by grimboid. Check out his great selection of sport, movie, TV and music posters at:

https://www.etsy.com/shop/headfuzzbygrimboid

Introduction

Think you know about the Kansas City Chiefs? Put your knowledge to the test with this selection of quizzes on all things red and gold.

The book covers the whole history of the franchise, from the early days under Hank Stram through to the recent revival under Andy Reid.

The biggest names in Chiefs history are present and correct so look out for questions on Derrick Thomas, Alex Smith, Christian Okoye, Kareem Hunt, Trent Green, Eric Berry and many, many more.

There are 500 questions in all covering running backs and receivers, coaches and quarterbacks, pass rushers and punters and much else besides.

Each quiz contains a selection of 20 questions and is either a mixed bag of pot luck testers or is centered on a specific category such as the 1990s or defense.

There are easy, medium and hard questions offering something for Chiefs novices as well as connoisseurs of Kansas City history.

You'll find the answers to each quiz below the bottom of the following quiz. For example, the answers to Quiz 1: Quarterbacks are underneath Quiz 2: Pot Luck. The only exception is Quiz 25: Anagrams. The answers to these can be found under the Quiz 1 questions.

All statistics relate to the regular season only unless otherwise stated and are accurate to the start of the 2017 season.

We hope you enjoy the Kansas City Trivia Quiz Book.

About the Author

Chris Bradshaw has written 17 quiz books including titles for Britain's biggest selling daily newspaper, The Sun, and The Times (of London). In addition to the NFL, he has written extensively on soccer, cricket, darts and poker.

He lives in Birmingham, England and has been following the NFL for over 30 years.

Acknowledgements

Many thanks to Ken and Veronica Bradshaw, Heidi Grant, Steph, James, Ben and Will Roe and Graham Nash.

CONTENTS

Quiz 1: Quarterbacks

1. Alex Smith joined the Chiefs following a trade with which team?

2. Which quarterback did the Chiefs select in the first round of the 2017 NFL Draft?

3. With 28,507 yards, who is Kansas City's all-time leading passer?

4. Which Hall of Famer was 17-8 as a starter in his two seasons with the Chiefs in 1993 and 1994?

5. What number jersey was worn by legendary quarterback Len Dawson?

6. Who are the three Chiefs quarterbacks to throw for over 4,000 yards in a season?

7. Who are the three Kansas City quarterbacks to appear in the Pro Bowl more than once?

8. Who is the only Chiefs quarterback to throw four touchdown passes in a single playoff game?

9. Which quarterback did the Chiefs select in the first round of the famous 1983 NFL Draft?

10. Who holds the record for the most 300-yard passing games in franchise history?

11. Which quarterback steered the Chiefs to a 10-6 record and a playoff appearance in 2010?

12. Who threw for a franchise record 504 yards against Oakland in 2000?

13. Who holds the record for the most interceptions in a single season after throwing 24 in 2001?

14. Of players with over 1,000 passing attempts for the Chiefs, who has the best completion percentage?

15. Which backup quarterback threw four interceptions in a 1992 playoff loss to the Bills?

16. Who is the only Chiefs quarterback to lead the league in passing yards?

17. In 1983, who set the franchise record for the most passing attempts in a season with 603?

18. In 2016, Alex Smith tied the record for the most rushing TDs by a Chiefs quarterback in a single season. Which quarterback also scored five TDs in 1995?

19. Between 1999 and 2000, Elvis Grbac threw touchdown passes in how many straight games? a) 13 b) 14 c) 15

20. In 2015, Alex Smith threw how many consecutive passes without an interception? a) 302 b) 312 c) 322

Quiz 25: Answers

1. Alex Smith 2. Andy Reid 3. Travis Kelce 4. Trent Green 5. Kareem Hunt 6. Hank Stram 7. Len Dawson 8. Priest Holmes 9. Tony Gonzalez 10. Dwayne Bowe 11. Neil Smith 12. Derrick Thomas 13. Nick Lowery 14. Cairo Santos 15. Otis Taylor 16. Marcus Peters 17. Marcus Allen 18. Eric Fisher 19. Willie Roaf 20. Jamaal Charles

Quiz 2: Pot Luck

1. Who are the two Chiefs tight ends with over 50 catches in three or more seasons?

2. What number jersey was worn by star linebacker Derrick Thomas?

3. The Chiefs wear what color helmets?

4. Which defensive tackle threw his first career touchdown pass during a Christmas Day 2016 rout of the Broncos?

5. Is the playing surface at Arrowhead made of grass or artificial turf?

6. Which receiver caught a touchdown pass in seven successive games in 2010?

7. In week 12 of the 2016 season, which Chief became the first NFL player since 1965 to score a rushing, receiving and return touchdown in the same game?

8. Which Chicago great was the last player to manage that feat?

9. The Chiefs overturned a franchise-record 21-point deficit in September 2016, going on to beat which division rival 33-27?

10. Chiefs running back Kareem Hunt played college ball at which school?

11. True or false – Elvis Grbac had more 300-yard passing games with the Chiefs than Joe Montana?

12. What color jerseys did the Chiefs wear while winning Super Bowl IV?

13. Who is the only Chiefs quarterback to have thrown six touchdown passes in a single game?

14. Who are the four Chiefs to record double-digit sacks in at least three seasons?

15. Which head coach holds the franchise record for the most wins in his first two seasons with the Chiefs?

16. What is the name of the Chiefs' horse mascot?

17. What jersey number was worn by star running back Christian Okoye?

18. 'Nick the Kick' was the nickname of which prolific Chiefs kicker?

19. In which round of the 1987 NFL Draft did the Chiefs select running back Christian Okoye? a) second b) seventh c) twelfth

20. What was the nickname of offensive lineman Willie Roaf? a) Mean b) Nasty c) Wicked

Quiz 1: Answers

1. San Francisco 2. Patrick Mahomes 3. Len Dawson 4. Joe Montana 5. #16 6. Len Dawson, Trent Green and Elvis Grbac 7. Len Dawson, Trent Green, Alex Smith 8. Alex Smith 9. Todd Blackledge 10. Trent Green 11. Matt Cassel 12. Elvis Grbac 13. Trent Green 14. Alex Smith 15. Mark Vlasic 16. Len Dawson 17. Bill Kenney 18. Steve Bono 19. c) 15 20. b) 312

Quiz 3: Running Backs

1. Who is Kansas City's all-time leading rusher?

2. Which legendary Chiefs running back was known as 'The Nigerian Nightmare'?

3. Which rookie running back rushed for 148 yards and a TD and caught five passes for 98 yards and another two TDs in the 2017 season opener against the Patriots?

4. In 2006, which Chiefs back set the NFL record for the most rushing attempts in a season with 406?

5. In January 2010, Jamaal Charles set the franchise record for the most rushing yards in a game against which division rival?

6. How many yards did Charles amass in that historic game?

7. Which Hall of Famer rushed for 3,698 yards in a spell in Kansas City that stretched from 1993 to 1997?

8. With 500 career points, which running back is the highest scoring non-kicker in franchise history?

9. True or false – Chiefs running back Christian Okoye appeared on the CBS reality TV show 'Pirate Master'?

10. Whose 1,789 rushing yards are the most by a Chiefs back in a single season?

11. In 1994, the Chiefs used their first-round draft pick to select which Texas A&M back?

12. In 1981, who became the first Chief to rush for over 1,000 yards in his rookie season?

13. Of Chiefs backs with over 400 carries, who has the best yards per rush average?

14. In which round of the 2017 NFL Draft did the Chiefs select Kareem Hunt?

15. Who holds the record for the most career rushing yards in playoff games for the Chiefs?

16. Which running back set a Chiefs rookie record after rushing for 10 touchdowns in 1981?

17. Who holds the record for the most 100-yard rushing games in Chiefs history?

18. Which Chiefs rookie rushed for 150 yards in a 2007 game against the Raiders?

19. Who holds the record for the most rushing touchdowns in a single season? a) Jamaal Charles b) Priest Holmes c) Christian Okoye

20. How many touchdowns did he score in that record-breaking season? a) 25 b) 26 c) 27

Quiz 2: Answers

1. Tony Gonzalez and Travis Kelce 2. #58 3. Red 4. Dontari Poe 5. Grass 6. Dwayne Bowe 7. Tyreek Hill 8. Gale Sayers 9. San Diego 10. University of Toledo 11. True 12. Red 13. Len Dawson 14. Derrick Thomas, Neil Smith, Justin Houston and Tamba Hali 15. Andy Reid 16. Warpaint 17. #35 18. Nick Lowery 19. a) Second 20. b) Nasty

Quiz 4: Pot Luck

1. Jamaal Charles tied a franchise record after scoring five touchdowns in a 2013 game against which team?

2. Which Chief has won the AFC Player of the Week Award the most times in franchise history

3. The Chiefs blew a 28-point lead to which team in the 2013 Wild Card playoff, eventually losing 45-44?

4. What number jersey is worn by star linebacker Derrick Johnson?

5. The Chiefs home jersey is made up of which three colors?

6. Which guard's 224 appearances between 1993 and 2006 are the most in franchise history?

7. Of Chiefs quarterbacks with over 1,000 attempts, who has the highest passer rating?

8. The Chiefs traded the 34th pick of the 2009 NFL Draft to the Patriots to acquire the services of which quarterback and linebacker?

9. Between 1991 and 2005 which quartet of Chiefs running backs won the AFC Player of the Month Award?

10. The Chiefs made their debut in London in 2015. Which team did they defeat at Wembley 45-10?

11. True or false – Chiefs kicker Nick Lowery had been cut by eight teams before joining Kansas City?

12. Legendary defensive lineman Curley Culp wore what number jersey?

13. Which quarterback enjoyed more wins with the Chiefs – Matt Cassel or Elvis Grbac?

14. Derrick Thomas holds the franchise record for reaching 30 sacks in the fewest number of games. Who is second on that list?

15. What is the name of the Chiefs' furry mascot?

16. True or false – In his stellar career with the Chiefs, Christian Okoye caught just 42 passes?

17. What number jersey is worn by linebacker Tamba Hali?

18. Which quarterback was sacked a franchise record 10 times in a 1980 game against Baltimore?

19. Which team did the Chiefs defeat in the AFL Championship Game to reach Super Bowl I? a) Boston b) Buffalo c) Denver

20. Which of the following receivers had the most receiving yards with the Chiefs? a) Dwayne Bowe b) Carlos Carson c) Stephone Paige

Quiz 3: Answers

1. Jamaal Charles 2. Christian Okoye 3. Kareem Hunt 4. Larry Johnson 5. Denver 6. 259 7. Marcus Allen 8. Priest Holmes 9. True 10. Larry Johnson 11. Greg Hill 12. Joe Delaney 13. Jamaal Charles 14. Third 15. Marcus Allen 16. Billy Jackson 17. Larry Johnson 18. Kolby Smith 19. b) Priest Holmes 20. c) 27

Quiz 5: Receivers

1. With 916 receptions, who is Kansas City's all-time leading receiver?

2. Whose 1,391 yards in 2000 are the most by a Chiefs receiver in a single season?

3. Which running back caught four touchdown passes in a 2013 game in Oakland?

4. Whose 481 yards between 1965 and 1975 are the most by a Chiefs receiver in playoff games?

5. Which former Chiefs tight end has the same name as the main character in TV drama 'Breaking Bad'?

6. Tony Gonzalez heads the list of most catches by a Chiefs tight end. Who is second on that list?

7. With 532 catches, who is the most prolific wide receiver in franchise history?

8. Tony Gonzalez is one of three Chiefs receivers with three or more 1,000-yard seasons. Who are the other two?

9. Which receiver, who spent three seasons in Kansas City in the late 1990s, was nicknamed 'Spider Man'?

10. Who holds the record for the most 100-yard receiving games in franchise history?

11. True or false – No Chiefs rookie has enjoyed a 1,000-yard receiving season?

12. Who caught eight catches for a franchise-record 309 yards against the Broncos in December 1985?

13. Whose 87 catches in 2015 were the most in a season by any Chiefs receiver not called Tony Gonzalez?

14. Whose 70 catches in 2007 are the most by a Chiefs rookie?

15. Whose 369 catches between 1991 and 2000 are the most by a Chiefs running back?

16. Whose 20 catches in 2002 resulted in a haul of eight touchdowns?

17. Of Chiefs receivers with over 200 catches, who has the best yards per catch average?

18. Who caught a 79-yard touchdown pass in the 2013 Wild Card round against the Colts?

19. What is the fewest number of passing yards the Chiefs have amassed in a game? a) -15 b) 5 c) 15

20. Between 2000 and 2008 Tony Gonzalez caught a pass in how many consecutive games? a) 111 b) 121 c) 131

Quiz 4: Answers

1. Oakland 2. Derrick Thomas 3. Indianapolis 4. #56 5. Red, white and gold 6. Will Shields 7. Alex Smith 8. Matt Cassel and Mike Vrabel 9. Christian Okoye, Barry Word, Priest Holmes and Larry Johnson 10. Detroit 11. True 12. #61 13. Elvis Grbac 14. Justin Houston 15. KC Wolf 16. True 17. #91 18. Steve Fuller 19. b) Buffalo 20. a) Dwayne Bowe

Quiz 6: Pot Luck

1. With 76 career touchdowns, who is the Chiefs' highest scoring pass catcher?

2. Which former Chiefs defensive great was a co-owner of the Kansas City Command Arena League franchise?

3. Quarterback Alex Smith played college ball at which school?

4. Who caught a 99-yard touchdown pass against the Chargers in December 2002?

5. Who threw that record-breaking pass?

6. Which tough offensive lineman, who spent four years with the Chiefs in the early 2000s, was inducted into the Pro Football Hall of Fame in 2012?

7. Who are the three Chiefs backs to rush for over 200 yards in a game?

8. Which former Chiefs all-time great is the owner of a gym called 68's Inside Sports?

9. Who returned a punt for a 95-yard touchdown against the Chargers on New Year's Day 2017?

10. Which Kansas City defensive back picked off eight passes in his 2015 rookie season?

11. Who is the only Chiefs quarterback to throw more than 50 passes in a game without an interception?

12. Lasting over 82 minutes, the longest playoff game in NFL history involved the Chiefs and which team?

13. True or false – In 2015 Arrowhead played host to an international soccer match between Mexico and Paraguay?

14. Which safety was the only Chiefs defender named on the NFL's All-Decade Team of the 1980s?

15. True or false – The Chiefs have never worn white jerseys in a game at Arrowhead?

16. In the 2005 season Larry Johnson rushed for over 100 yards in how many successive games?

17. Which quarterback won his only game as a starter for the Chiefs, defeating the Jaguars in November 2016?

18. In which round of the 2013 draft did the Chiefs select tight end Travis Kelce?

19. What is the highest ever attendance for a Chiefs regular season home game? a) 80,893 b) 81,893 c) 82,893

20. In 2002, Priest Holmes set a franchise record after scoring a touchdown in how many straight games? a) 10 b) 11 c) 12

Quiz 5: Answers

1. Tony Gonzalez 2. Derrick Alexander 3. Jamaal Charles 4. Otis Taylor 5. Walter White 6. Travis Kelce 7. Dwayne Bowe 8. Carlos Carson and Dwayne Bowe 9. Andre Rison 10. Tony Gonzalez 11. True 12. Stephone Paige 13. Jeremy Maclin 14. Dwayne Bowe 15. Kimble Anders 16. Marc Boerigter 17. Carlos Carson 18. Donnie Avery 19. a) -15 20. c) 131

Quiz 7: Defense

1. Who is the Chiefs' all-time leader in sacks?

2. Who is second on the all-time sacks list?

3. Which defensive superstar did the Chiefs select with the fifth overall pick of the 2010 NFL Draft?

4. Which team did the Chiefs shut out in a January 2016 playoff game?

5. Who holds the franchise record for the most sacks in a single season?

6. How many sacks did he record to set that record?

7. Which Chiefs defensive back intercepted three passes in a game against Miami in 2002 and three more against the Patriots in 2005?

8. Which defender returned an interception 38 yards for a touchdown against Oakland in December 2015 then ran in a fumble 73 yards for another touchdown against Baltimore two weeks later?

9. Which alliteratively-named cornerback returned an interception 100 yards for a touchdown against Buffalo in November 2013?

10. Which two Kansas City defenders were named on the NFL All-Decade Team for the 1990s?

11. Who is the Chiefs' all-time leading tackler?

12. Derrick Thomas is one of two Chiefs with 6.5 postseason sacks. Who is the other?

13. In 2008, the Chiefs set the NFL record for recording the fewest sacks in a single season. How many times did they sack opposition quarterbacks that year?

14. Which Chiefs linebacker forced a record six fumbles in his rookie season in 2006?

15. Whose 58 interceptions between 1966 and 1978 are a Chiefs franchise record?

16. Which defensive lineman's nine sacks in 2007 were the second most by a Chiefs rookie in franchise history?

17. Who returned two interceptions for touchdowns against the Broncos in January 2010?

18. In December 2009, the Chiefs gave up a franchise record 351 rushing yards in a game against which AFC North team?

19. What is the fewest total yards the Chiefs defense has given up in a single game? a) 79 yards b) 89 yards c) 99 yards

20. How many fumbles did Derrick Thomas force during his stellar career? a) 25 b) 35 c) 45

Quiz 6: Answers

1. Tony Gonzalez 2. Neil Smith 3. University of Utah 4. Marc Boerigter 5. Trent Green 6. Willie Roaf 7. Jamaal Charles, Larry Johnson and Barry Word 8. Will Shields 9. Tyreek Hill 10. Marcus Peters 11. Matt Cassel 12. Miami 13. True 14. Deron Cherry 15. False 16. Nine 17. Nick Foles 18. Third 19. c) 82,893 20. b) 11

Quiz 8: Pot Luck

1. Quarterback Patrick Mahomes played college football at which school?

2. Justin Houston sacked which Philadelphia quarterback 4.5 times in a September 2013 game against the Eagles?

3. 'The Black Mamba' is the nickname of which explosive receiver and returner?

4. Who holds the franchise record for the most rushing yards by a quarterback in a single season with 498?

5. What retired jersey number was worn by star defensive back Emmitt Thomas?

6. Who was the only Chiefs running back to have a 100-yard rushing game in 2016?

7. The award given to Kansas City's Player of the Year is named after which former star?

8. Which Chief was named AFC Player of the Month for September 2017?

9. Which running back caught an 80-yard touchdown pass against Denver in November 2015?

10. Which quarterback threw a record-breaking six interceptions in a 1985 loss to the Rams?

11. Which quarterback won more games as a starter for the Chiefs – Joe Montana or Steve Bono?

12. True or false – Despite winning just two games in 2012 the Chiefs sent six players to the Pro Bowl?

13. Which undrafted free agent from a division rival holds the record for the most 100-yard receiving games against the Chiefs?

14. Who is Kansas City's all-time leading points scorer in playoff games?

15. Who returned punts for 94 and 89-yard touchdowns against the Chargers and Giants in 2010 and 2013?

16. What number jersey is worn by explosive runner and receiver Tyreek Hill?

17. True or false – Marv Levy never enjoyed a winning season while head coach of the Chiefs?

18. Chiefs great Neil Smith won two Super Bowl rings with which team?

19. How long is the longest run in Chiefs history? a) 91 yards b) 92 yards c) 93 yards

20. Who scored a touchdown on that record-breaking score? a) Jamaal Charles b) Priest Holmes c) Barry Word

Quiz 7: Answers

1. Derrick Thomas 2. Tamba Hali 3. Eric Berry 4. Houston 5. Justin Houston 6. 22 sacks 7. Greg Wesley 8. Tyvon Branch 9. Sean Smith 10. Neil Smith and Derrick Thomas 11. Derrick Johnson 12. Neil Smith 13. Just 10 times 14. Tamba Hali 15. Emmitt Thomas 16. Jared Allen 17. Derrick Johnson 18. Cleveland 19. b) 88 yards 20. c) 45

Quiz 9: Special Teams

1. With 1,466 points, who is Kansas City's all-time leading points scorer?

2. Who returned two punts and one kickoff for touchdowns during his 2016 rookie year?

3. Whose 108-yard kickoff return against the Broncos in January 2013 is the longest in franchise history?

4. In what country was kicker Cairo Santos born?

5. Who has been the Chiefs special teams coordinator since 2013?

6. Which explosive returner scored five punt return and six kickoff-return touchdowns between 2000 and 2006?

7. Since the 1970 merger, who is the only Chiefs kicker to be a perfect 100% on PAT attempts?

8. Which cornerback blocked 10 punts during a stellar career that ran from 1983 until 1993?

9. Who holds the record for the longest converted field goal in team history?

10. How long was that record-breaking field goal?

11. Which kicker's 517 points between 2009 and 2013 are good enough for third place on the Chiefs' all-time scoring list?

12. True or false – Former Chiefs kicker Lawrence Tynes was born in Ireland?

13. Whose 139 points are the most recorded by a Chiefs kicker in a single season?

14. Who holds the record for the most successful field goals in a single game with seven?

15. In 1997 and 1998, who set the franchise record for the most consecutive field goals made after connecting on 22 in a row?

16. Who tied that streak record in 2011?

17. Which kicker, who spent two seasons in Kansas City in the early 2000s, was inducted into the Pro Football Hall of Fame in 2017?

18. Kicker Jan Stenerud was the first player from which country to play in the NFL?

19. Who holds the record for the longest punt in franchise history? a) Dustin Colquitt b) Bob Grupp c) Dan Stryzinski

20. How long was that record-breaking punt? a) 77 yards b) 79 yards c) 81 yards

Quiz 8: Answers

1. Texas Tech 2. Michael Vick 3. De'Anthony Thomas 4. Alex Smith 5. #18 6. Spencer Ware 7. Derrick Thomas 8. Kareem Hunt 9. Charcandrick West 10. Todd Blackledge 11. Steve Bono 12. True 13. Rod Smith 14. Nick Lowery 15. Dexter McCluster 16. #10 17. False 18. Denver 19. a) 91 yards 20. a) Jamaal Charles

Quiz 10: Pot Luck

1. Who holds the record for the most yards from scrimmage in franchise history?

2. Which defensive superstar is the only Chief to play in three different decades?

3. Between 1990 and 2016, who were the two Kansas City quarterbacks to win the AFC Player of the Month award?

4. Which Chiefs Hall of Fame defensive lineman was an NCAA heavyweight wrestling champion?

5. True or false – In 1977, the Chiefs defense allowed on average over 200 rushing yards per game?

6. Which Hall of Fame quarterback played the final game of his pro career for the Chiefs in 2000?

7. Which Kansas City linebacker was named the Defensive MVP of the 2013 Pro Bowl?

8. Who holds the franchise record for scoring the most points in a single season?

9. What is the name of punter Dustin Colquitt's brother who is also an NFL punter?

10. The award given to the Chiefs' Rookie of the Year is named after which former player?

11. True or false – Chiefs defensive coach Bob Sutton spent nine years as head coach of Navy?

12. The Chiefs defeated the Falcons in 2015 after which defensive back intercepted a two-point conversion attempt and ran it back for a score?

13. What number jersey did star rusher Jamaal Charles wear?

14. Which Kansas City full back went to the Pro Bowl in both 2003 and 2004?

15. The #36 jersey is retired in honor of which 1960s era running back?

16. True or false – In a 1965 game against Denver, the Chiefs amassed a franchise low of zero rushing yards?

17. Who are the two Chiefs kickers to boot four 50-yard or more field goals in a single season?

18. Which quarterback has rushed for the most yards in Chiefs history?

19. What is the most points that the Chiefs have given up in a single season? a) 420 b) 430 c) 440

20. The longest winning run in franchise history stretched to how many games? a) 10 b) 11 c) 12

Quiz 9: Answers

1. Nick Lowery 2. Tyreek Hill 3. Knile Davis 4. Brazil 5. Dave Toub 6. Dante Hall 7. Ryan Succop 8. Albert Lewis 9. Nick Lowery 10. 58 yards 11. Ryan Succop 12. False (he was born in Scotland) 13. Nick Lowery 14. Cairo Santos 15. Pete Stoyanovich 16. Ryan Succop 17. Morten Andersen 18. Norway 19. a) Dustin Colquitt 20. c) 81 yards

Quiz 11: 1960s and 70s

1. Which team did the Chiefs defeat to win Super Bowl IV?

2. What was the score in that game?

3. Super Bowl IV took place in which stadium?

4. Who was the MVP in Super Bowl IV?

5. The Chiefs reached Super Bowl IV after defeating which team in the AFL Championship Game?

6. The Chiefs franchise was founded by which legendary figure?

7. Who set an NFL record in 1972 after returning four interceptions for a touchdown?

8. The Chiefs franchise started life in which city?

9. In 1976, who became the first Chiefs player to lead the NFL in receptions?

10. In what year did the Kansas City Chiefs play their first game?

11. Which alliterative Kansas City defensive star was named a First-Team All-Pro six times and went to the Pro Bowl nine times between 1964 and 1972?

12. In what year did the Chiefs play their first game at Arrowhead?

13. The Chiefs suffered a heart-breaking double overtime loss to which team in the divisional round playoff on Christmas Day 1971?

14. Which defensive back's 12 picks in 1974 are the most by a Chief in a single season?

15. Which team did the Chiefs face in the first ever Super Bowl?

16. That maiden Super Bowl was hosted at which famous stadium?

17. 'Honey Bear' was the nickname of which fearsome Chiefs defender who played in Kansas City from 1967 until 1977?

18. Who was the only Chiefs quarterback to go to the Pro Bowl throughout the whole of the 1970s?

19. How many straight losing seasons did the Chiefs endure in the 1970s? a) 4 b) 5 c) 6

20. How many division titles did the Chiefs win during the 1970s? a) none b) one c) two

Quiz 10: Answers

1. Tony Gonzalez 2. Derrick Thomas 3. Steve DeBerg and Matt Cassel 4. Curley Culp 5. True 6. Warren Moon 7. Derrick Johnson 8. Priest Holmes 9. Britton 10. Mack Lee Hill 11. False – he coached Army 12. Eric Berry 13. #25 14. Tony Richardson 15. Mack Lee Hill 16. True 17. Nick Lowery and Cairo Santos 18. Alex Smith 19. c) 440 20. b) 11

Quiz 12: Pot Luck

1. Which two-time Super Bowl-winning head coach was the backup quarterback on Kansas City's Super Bowl IV championship roster?

2. Star defensive lineman Neil Smith wore what number jersey?

3. Which Chiefs defender won the Walter Payton Man of the Year Award in 1993?

4. After leaving the Chiefs, Marty Schottenheimer's next head coaching job was with which team?

5. Which legendary Chiefs defender has been the team's defensive backs coach since 2010?

6. Who in 2002 became the first Chiefs kick returner to go to the Pro Bowl in more than 20 years?

7. Which running back had more 100-yard rushing games with the Chiefs – Marcus Allen or Barry Word?

8. True or false – The Chiefs have had a representative at the Pro Bowl every year since its inception?

9. Which Chiefs receiver, drafted in 2014, played Pop Warner football on a team coached by rapper Snoop Dogg?

10. Which Chief released a single in 2017 produced by Masterkraft entitled 'The One For Me'?

11. Tight end Travis Kelce played college ball at which school?

12. Which quarterback had a starting record of 31-20-1 in his spell with the Chiefs between 1988 and 1991?

13. True or false – Pro Bowl safety Deron Cherry originally joined the Chiefs as a free agent punter?

14. 'The Rock' was the nickname of which cornerback who played 156 games for the Chiefs between 1984 and 1993?

15. True or false – The Chiefs were the first AFL team to win a Super Bowl?

16. Before moving to Arrowhead, what stadium did the Chiefs call home?

17. What number jersey was worn by star kicker Jan Stenerud?

18. The Chiefs were beaten 3-0 in a 1979 game against which NFC team?

19. Who was the Chiefs starting quarterback in their only playoff appearance in the 1980s? a) Todd Blackledge b) Steve DeBerg c) Bill Kenney

20. In which country was Chiefs kicker Nick Lowery born? a) France b) Italy c) Germany

Quiz 11: Answers

1. Minnesota 2. Vikings 7-24 Chiefs 3. Tulane Stadium 4. Len Dawson 5. Oakland 6. Lamar Hunt 7. Jim Kearney 8. Dallas 9. MacArthur Lane 10. 1963 11. Bobby Bell 12. 1972 13. Miami 14. Emmitt Thomas 15. Green Bay 16. Los Angeles Memorial Coliseum 17. Willie Lanier 18. Len Dawson 19. c) 6 20. b) One

Quiz 13: 1980s

1. Who, in 1989, became the first Chief to lead the NFL in rushing?

2. In 1981, who became the first Chiefs rookie running back to go to the Pro Bowl?

3. The Chiefs started the 1980s with which future Hall of Famer as head coach?

4. Which All-Pro defensive end led the team in sacks in 1980, 1982, 1984 and 1986?

5. Who was the only Chiefs receiver with over 1,000 receiving yards in a season during the 1980s?

6. Which 12th round draft pick won 34 games as Kansas City's starting quarterback between 1980 and 1988?

7. The Chiefs reached the postseason just once during the 1980s. Which head coach steered them to the 1986 playoffs?

8. The Chiefs defeated which team 24-19 in the 1986 season finale with all their points coming via special teams?

9. Whose 10 interceptions in 1980 put him in second place on the most picks in a season in franchise history list?

10. Which Chiefs nose tackle was named the AP NFL Defensive Rookie of the Year in 1984?

11. Which team eliminated the 1986 Chiefs from the playoffs in the Wild Card round?

12. Which veteran quarterback's first pass for the Chiefs was intercepted and returned for a touchdown against Denver in 1989?

13. Who picked off four passes in a 1985 game against Seattle?

14. Which defensive superstar did the Chiefs select with the third overall pick of the 1988 NFL Draft?

15. Which safety returned two interceptions for touchdowns in a game against the Chargers in October 1986?

16. The Chiefs lost a wild 1983 shoot-out 51-48 to which team?

17. True or false – The final game of the 1983 season against Denver attracted a crowd of just 11,377?

18. How many division titles did the Chiefs win during the 1980s?

19. What was the most wins recorded by the Chiefs during a single season in the 1980s? a) 9 b) 10 c) 11

20. The Chiefs set a franchise record after recording how many sacks against the Browns in September 1984? a) 9 b) 10 c) 11

Quiz 12: Answers

1. Tom Flores 2. #90 3. Derrick Thomas 4. Washington 5. Emmitt Thomas 6. Dante Hall 7. Barry Word 8. False 9. De'Anthony Thomas 10. Tamba Hali 11. Cincinnati 12. Steve Deberg 13. True 14. Kevin Ross 15. False 16. Municipal Stadium 17. #3 18. Tampa Bay 19. a) Todd Blackledge 20. b) Germany

Quiz 14: Pot Luck

1. Which running back was named the NFL's Offensive Player of the Year in 2002?

2. Who has been the 'Voice of the Chiefs' on Kansas City radio game broadcasts since 1994?

3. @superdj56 is the Twitter handle of which Chiefs defender?

4. Who were the two Kansas City running backs to rush for over 1,000 yards in a season during the 1980s?

5. Who are the three Chiefs to lead the NFL in single-season sacks?

6. Between 1996 and 2015 the Governor's Cup was awarded to the winners of games between the Chiefs and which team?

7. In 2003, who became the first Chiefs quarterback to register a 'perfect' 158.3 passer rating in a game?

8. The Chiefs used the first overall pick of the 2013 NFL Draft to select which offensive lineman?

9. Which former Chief is the author of a book called 'The All-Pro Diet: Lose Fat, Build Muscle, and Live Like a Champion'?

10. True or false – Arrowhead once played host to the annual Pro Bowl game?

11. Who returned a punt for a game-winning 93-yard touchdown in the closing stages of a 2003 game against Denver?

12. In August 2017, the Chiefs acquired linebacker Reggie Ragland following a trade with which team?

13. Which quarterback was 2-1 as starter with the Chiefs in 2011, including a 7-3 win over his former team, Denver?

14. True or false – Chiefs defensive back Daniel Sorensen was born in Denmark?

15. What specialist position on the 2017 Chiefs roster was held by James Winchester?

16. Which alliteratively named linebacker was the first Chief inducted into the Pro Football Hall of Fame?

17. True or false – Will Shields never missed a game in his stellar 14-year career?

18. What is the name of Dustin Colquitt's father who won two Super Bowl rings as a punter with the Steelers?

19. Which former Chiefs quarterback served in the Missouri State Senate from 1994 until 2002? a) Steve DeBerg b) Elvis Grbac c) Bill Kenney

20. Derrick Thomas and Neil Smith combined for how many sacks during their time in Kansas City? a) 202.5 b) 212.5 c) 222.5

Quiz 13: Answers

1. Christian Okoye 2. Joe Delaney 3. Marv Levy 4. Art Still 5. Carlos Carson 6. Bill Kenney 7. John Mackovic 8. Pittsburgh 9. Gary Barbaro 10. Bill Maas 11. New York Jets 12. Steve DeBerg 13. Deron Cherry 14. Neil Smith 15. Lloyd Burruss 16. Seattle 17. True 18. None 19. b) 10 20. c) 11

Quiz 15: 1990s

1. Who were the two Chiefs running backs to rush for over 1,000 yards in a season during the 1990s?

2. The Chiefs thrashed which defending AFC champion 33-6 in a 1991 Monday Night Football game?

3. In December 1991, the Chiefs defeated which division rival to secure a first playoff win since Super Bowl IV?

4. The Chiefs had two head coaches during the 1990s. Can you name them?

5. The 1993 Chiefs lost in the AFC Championship game to which team?

6. Which Chiefs running back was named the Pro Football Weekly Comeback Player of the Year in 1993?

7. Which first-round draft pick scored a 46-yard punt return touchdown with his first touch as a pro against the Chargers in 1992?

8. Which quarterback scrambled his way to a 76-yard touchdown run against the Cardinals in October 1995?

9. On Thanksgiving Day 1996, which Chief broke the NFL record for the most career rushing touchdowns?

10. True or false – In 1999, the Chiefs defense ran in nine touchdowns?

11. Who returned four punts and four kickoffs for touchdowns between 1995 and 1999?

12. The Chiefs routed which team 44-9 at Arrowhead in November 1997 to abruptly end an 11-game winning streak?

13. Which alliteratively-named Chief led the AFC in interceptions in 1997 with nine, returning three of the them for touchdowns?

14. Which two 1990s-era players are the only Chiefs defensive backs to win the AFC Player of the Month Award?

15. Derrick Thomas and Neil Smith were two of the three Chiefs to lead the team in single-season sacks in the 1990s. Who, in 1997, was the third?

16. In 1997, who became the first Chiefs receiver to make the Pro Bowl in more than a decade?

17. Which full back led the team in receptions in 1994, 1995, 1996 and 1998?

18. What was the most wins recorded by the Chiefs in a single regular season in the 1990s?

19. The 1997 Chiefs set the franchise record for the fewest points allowed in a 16-game season conceding how many? a) 232 b) 242 c) 252

20. How many times did the Chiefs reach the playoffs during the 1990s? a) five b) six c) seven

Quiz 14: Answers

1. Priest Holmes 2. Mitch Holthus 3. Derrick Johnson 4. Joe Delaney and Christian Okoye 5. Derrick Thomas, Neil Smith and Jared Allen 6. St Louis Rams 7. Trent Green 8. Eric Fisher 9. Tony Gonzalez 10. True 11. Dante Hall 12. Buffalo 13. Kyle Orton 14. False 15. Long snapper 16. Bobby Bell 17. True 18. Craig 19. c) Bill Kenney 20. b) 212.5

Quiz 16: Pot Luck

1. With which pick of the 1989 NFL Draft did the Chiefs select star linebacker Derrick Thomas?

2. Derrick Thomas recorded seven sacks in a dominating defensive display against which team in November 1990?

3. Which quarterback, who later played for the Chiefs, was on the receiving end of those seven sacks?

4. Which former quarterback is the regular color commentator on Chiefs Radio Network broadcasts?

5. Since 2000, the Chiefs have picked a wide receiver in the first round of the NFL Draft three times. Which trio did they select?

6. In 2011, who became the first pair of Kansas City linebackers to be elected to the Pro Bowl in the same year since the 1972 season?

7. True or false – Marcus Allen never enjoyed a 1,000-yard rushing season with the Chiefs?

8. Which quarterback, who was with the Chiefs from 2007 until 2009, won just one of his 11 games as a starter?

9. Did Trent Green have a winning or losing record as a starter with the Chiefs?

10. 'Mighty Mouse' was the nickname of which diminutive defensive back who played in Kansas City in the late 1990s?

11. True or false – Quarterback Patrick Mahomes was drafted by the Detroit Tigers in the 2014 MLB Draft?

12. What does the D in the name of defensive back D.J. White stand for?

13. Herthie is the unusual middle name of which former Chiefs great?

14. Which future All-Pro defensive lineman did the Chiefs select with the second overall pick of the 1978 NFL Draft?

15. In 1990, the Chiefs faced the Rams in an exhibition game at the Olympic Stadium in which European city?

16. The Chiefs hold their summer training camp at which local university?

17. Which two Chiefs were named on the NFL's 75th Anniversary Team?

18. Which Chiefs defender was named UPI's AFC Rookie of the Year in 1992?

19. The Chiefs are unbeaten in playoff games against which of the following teams? a) Buffalo b) Houston c) Miami

20. Pro Bowl full back Tony Richardson was born in which country? a) Great Britain b) Germany c) Japan

Quiz 15: Answers

1. Barry Word and Christian Okoye 2. Buffalo 3. L.A. Raiders 4. Marty Schottenheimer and Gunther Cunningham 5. Buffalo 6. Marcus Allen 7. Dale Carter 8. Steve Bono 9. Marcus Allen 10. True 11. Tamarick Vanover 12. San Francisco 13. Mark McMillian 14. James Hasty and Jerome Woods 15. Dan Williams 16. Andre Rison 17. Kimble Anders 18. 13 wins 19. a) 232 points 20. c) Seven times

Quiz 17: 2000s

1. Which Super Bowl winner was appointed the Chiefs head coach in January 2001?

2. The Chiefs defeated which defending Super Bowl champion 54-34 in a wild October 2000 game at Arrowhead?

3. Kansas City acquired quarterback Trent Green following a trade with which team?

4. The Chiefs shut out which team 49-0 in December 2002?

5. In 2003, which Chief became the first player in NFL history to return a kick for a touchdown in four straight games?

6. True or false – despite leading the NFL in points scored in 2002 with 467, the Chiefs failed to record a winning record?

7. In 2001, who became the second chief to win the NFL rushing title?

8. The 2002 and 2003 Chiefs were the first team to lead the AFC in scoring in successive seasons in over 20 years. What pass-happy team was the last to manage that feat?

9. In 2008, the Chiefs traded star defensive lineman Jared Allen to which team?

10. Which linebacker led the team in sacks in 2006, 2008 and 2009?

11. In 2004, the Chiefs became the first team in NFL history to have three different backs rush for over 150 yards in a game in the same season. Can you name the trio?

12. Which former scout and assistant was named Kansas City head coach in January 2006?

13. Which quarterback had a starting record of 10 wins and 11 losses with the Chiefs between 2006 and 2008?

14. Two Kansas City offensive linemen won the NFL Walter Payton Man of the Year Award in the 2000s. Which two?

15. The Chiefs shut out which NFC West team 41-0 in October 2006?

16. What was the most games won by the Chiefs in a single regular season during the 2000s?

17. What was the lowest number of games won by the Chiefs during a single season in the 2000s?

18. How many playoff games did the Chiefs win throughout the decade?

19. Why did the Chiefs play a 2005 game in Miami on a Friday night? a) There was a political convention in town b) There was a hurricane c) There was a clash with the World Series

20. The Chiefs set an NFL record in a 2004 game against Atlanta after rushing for how many touchdowns? a) six b) seven c) eight

Quiz 16: Answers

1. Fourth 2. Seattle 3. Dave Krieg 4. Len Dawson 5. Sylvester Morris, Dwayne Bowe and Jon Baldwin 6. Derrick Johnson and Tamba Hali 7. True 8. Tyler Thigpen 9. Winning 10. Mark McMillian 11. True 12. David 13. Will Shields 14. Art Still 15. Berlin 16. Missouri West State University 17. Willie Lanier and Jan Stenerud 18. Dale Carter 19. b) Houston 20. b) Germany

Quiz 18: Pot Luck

1. Which Kansas City defensive great has a brother called Dwight who played in the NFL with the Giants and Eagles in the early 2000s?

2. Who was the only Chiefs defender to receive First Team All-Pro honors during the 2000s?

3. Which defensive star's three safeties are the most in franchise history?

4. Which running back's only kickoff return touchdown was a 97-yard effort in an overtime win over Pittsburgh in 2009?

5. In which round of the 2016 NFL Draft did the Chiefs select explosive runner Tyreek Hill?

6. Which long-serving special teamer did the Chiefs select in the third round of the 2005 NFL Draft?

7. True or false – Defensive star Dee Ford is an accomplished piano player?

8. Which rookie cornerback picked off Houston's Brian Hoyer in his first regular season snap in 2015?

9. Who are the two Chiefs kickers since 1990 to have won the AFC Special Teams Player of the Month Award?

10. Which Chiefs general manager won the Pro Football Weekly Executive of the Year award in 2013?

11. Which former first round draft pick for the Browns was 1-7 as a starting quarterback with the Chiefs in 2012?

12. True or false – The miserly 1997 defense didn't give up a second-half touchdown in 10 successive games?

13. Who are the four starting quarterbacks to steer the Chiefs to a playoff win?

14. What is the name of Travis Kelce's brother who is an offensive lineman for the Eagles?

15. Which alliteratively named Kansas City defensive tackle was part of the 2013 Pro Football Hall of Fame class?

16. Which Chiefs running back tragically died following a knee operation in 1965?

17. Which 6ft 10in Chiefs tight end had a rule named after him that prevents players from batting down kicks underneath the crossbar?

18. With Marty Schottenheimer in charge, the Chiefs played the Raiders 21 times. How many of those games did Kansas City win?

19. What was the nickname of Chiefs defensive back Fred Williamson?
a) The Anvil b) The Hammer c) The Shotgun

20. What is the current capacity of Arrowhead? a) 72,416 b) 74,416 c) 76,416

Quiz 17: Answers

1. Dick Vermeil 2. St Louis Rams 3. St Louis Rams 4. Arizona 5. Dante Hall 6. True 7. Priest Holmes 8. San Diego 9. Minnesota 10. Tamba Hali 11. Priest Holmes, Larry Johnson and Derrick Blaylock 12. Herm Edwards 13. Damon Huard 14. Will Shields and Brian Waters 15. San Francisco 16. 13 games 17. Two games 18. None 19. b) There was a hurricane 20. c) Eight

Quiz 19: 2010s

1. The 2010 Chiefs were eliminated from the playoffs following a 30-7 home loss to which team?

2. In 2010, who set the franchise record for the most receiving touchdowns in a season with 15?

3. The Chiefs delivered a 28-0 road shutout in a 2011 game against which division rival?

4. Which kicker led the team in scoring every year between 2010 and 2013?

5. The Chiefs used the 11th overall pick of the 2012 NFL Draft to select which defensive tackle?

6. Before Tyreek Hill, who was the last Chief to return a punt for a touchdown?

7. Whose reign as general manager ended in 2013?

8. Who was replaced as the Chiefs head coach 13 games into the 2013 season?

9. The Chiefs ended the 2015 regular season by winning how many games in a row?

10. How many games did the Chiefs win in Romeo Crennel's only full season as head coach?

11. Who turned a short screen pass against the Broncos on Christmas Day 2016 into a memorable 80-yard touchdown?

12. Which much-traveled center made his 200th career start in the 2012 season finale?

13. True or false – The Chiefs sent more players to the 2013 Pro Bowl than any other team?

14. How many games did the Chiefs win in Andy Reid's first season as head coach?

15. Who returned a kickoff 106 yards for a touchdown in a historic 30-0 playoff win over the Texans?

16. Who was named the AP NFL Defensive Rookie of the Year in 2015?

17. What color jersey and pants combo did the Chiefs wear for the first time in franchise history against the Cowboys in 2013?

18. With 921 yards, who led the Chiefs in rushing in 2016?

19. The Chiefs defeated which team 28-2 in Andy Reid's first game as head coach? a) Jacksonville b) Miami c) Tennessee

20. Andy Reid started his tenure as Chiefs head coach by winning how many straight games? a) seven b) eight c) nine

Quiz 18: Answers

1. Derrick Johnson 2. Jared Allen 3. Derrick Thomas 4. Jamaal Charles 5. Fifth 6. Dustin Colquitt 7. True 8. Marcus Peters 9. Pete Stoyanovich and Cairo Santos 10. John Dorsey 11. Brady Quinn 12. True 13. Len Dawson, Joe Montana, Steve DeBerg, Alex Smith 14. Jason Kelce 15. Curley Culp 16. Mack Lee Hill 17. Morris Stroud 18. 18 19. b) The Hammer 20. c) 76,416

Quiz 20: Pot Luck

1. Which team eliminated the Chiefs from the 2016 playoffs despite not scoring a touchdown?

2. Which Chiefs star was named the offensive MVP in the 2017 Pro Bowl?

3. Which quarterback started 10 games for the Chiefs between 2006 and 2010 and was on the losing side every time?

4. Kansas City's first round draft picks in 2003 and 2005 shared the same surname. Which one?

5. True or false – The Chiefs were the first team to appear in the Super Bowl more than once?

6. After 12 seasons with the Chiefs Tony Gonzalez ended his career with which team?

7. In 2017, which Chief became the first player to score touchdowns of 50 yards or more in his first three NFL games?

8. Which Hall of Fame center, who won multiple Super Bowl rings, spent the final two years of his career in 1989 and 1990 with the Chiefs?

9. Do the Chiefs have a winning or losing record in games played at Arrowhead?

10. True or false – Quarterback Pat Mahomes in the son of a former 11-year MLB relief pitcher?

11. Before Alex Smith, who was the last quarterback to steer the Chiefs to a winning season?

12. Which two Chiefs backs each rushed for four touchdowns in a 2004 game against Atlanta?

13. Do the Chiefs have a winning or losing record in playoff games?

14. Which center played 169 games for the Chiefs between 1990 and 2000?

15. Which defensive back returned a kickoff 95 yards for a touchdown against Washington in 2013?

16. Who won more games with the Chiefs – Todd Blackledge or Matt Cassel?

17. Which Chiefs quarterback caught a touchdown pass in a 2008 game against the Bucs?

18. Which former Chiefs defensive back later enjoyed a successful acting career that included the starring role in the 1973 movie 'Black Caesar'?

19. What is the most consecutive seasons that the Chiefs have reached the playoffs? a) four b) five c) six

20. Defensive lineman Rakeen Nunez-Roches was born in which central American country? a) Belize b) Guatemala c) Honduras

Quiz 19: Answers

1. Baltimore 2. Dwayne Bowe 3. Oakland 4. Ryan Succop 5. Dontari Poe 6. De'Anthony Thomas 7. Scott Pioli 8. Todd Haley 9. Ten 10. Two 11. Travis Kelce 12. Casey Wiegmann 13. False 14. 11 games 15. Knile Davis 16. Marcus Peters 17. Red jersey and red pants 18. Spencer Ware 19. a) Jacksonville 20. c) Nine

Quiz 21: Coaches

1. Which head coach steered the Chiefs to world championship glory in Super Bowl IV?

2. Before taking charge of the Chiefs, Andy Reid spent 14 seasons with which team?

3. Before Andy Reid, who was the last Chiefs head coach to steer the team to the playoffs?

4. Which former quarterbacks coach was named Kansas City's offensive coordinator prior to the 2017 season?

5. After 13 years with the Jets, who became Kansas City's defensive coordinator in 2013?

6. In July 2017, which 39-year-old was appointed the Chiefs general manager, becoming the youngest person in that role in the NFL?

7. Hank Stram holds the franchise record for the most career wins. Who is second on that list?

8. Which former Seahawks, Redskins and Bears tackle has been the Chiefs o-line coach since 2013?

9. What name is missing from this list – Vermeil, Edwards, ????, Crennel?

10. Who are the three head coaches to have won a playoff game while with the Chiefs?

11. True or false – The Chiefs enjoyed a winning record in each of Andy Reid's first four seasons as head coach?

12. Which current NFC head coach spent three years as the offensive coordinator in Kansas City from 2013 through to 2015?

13. In 1998 and 1999 Andy Reid was the quarterbacks coach at which NFC North team?

14. Who won more games as Kansas City head coach – John Mackovic or Dick Vermeil?

15. Before being appointed head coach in Kansas City, Herm Edwards spent five seasons in charge of which team?

16. Which future Super Bowl winner turned pundit was KC's defensive coordinator in 1989, 1990 and 1991?

17. Chiefs assistant head coach Brad Childress had a spell as head coach at which NFC team?

18. Before becoming Chiefs head coach, Todd Haley was the offensive coordinator at which NFC champion?

19. How many regular season games did the Chiefs win with Hank Stram as head coach? a) 124 b) 134 c) 144

20. Up to the start of the 2017 season the Chiefs had had how many head coaches in franchise history? a) 11 b) 12 c) 13

Quiz 20: Answers

1. Pittsburgh 2. Travis Kelce 3. Brodie Croyle 4. Johnson 5. False 6. Atlanta 7. Kareem Hunt 8. Mike Webster 9. Winning 10. True 11. Matt Cassel 12. Priest Holmes and Derrick Blaylock 13. Losing 14. Tim Grunhard 15. Quintin Demps 16. Matt Cassel 17. Tyler Thigpen 18. Fred Williamson 19. c) Six 20. a) Belize

Quiz 22: Pot Luck

1. Which kicker is second on the Chiefs' all-time games played list?

2. Which quarterback started every game for the Chiefs between 2001 and 2005?

3. Which Chief was named AP's NFL Comeback Player of the Year for 2015?

4. Who are the four Chiefs to record 15 or more sacks in a single season?

5. The first sporting event at the revamped Arrowhead saw the Kansas City Wizards take on which English Premier League soccer team?

6. Which former Kansas City great is the host of a National Geographic TV show called 'You Can't Lick Your Elbow'?

7. The Chiefs have used a first-round draft choice the most times to pick a player in which position?

8. True or false – Alex Smith's father spent three seasons in the NFL as a backup quarterback?

9. Who holds the franchise record for the most Pro Bowl appearances while with the Chiefs?

10. How many times was he voted to the Pro Bowl to set that record?

11. Which former Seahawks quarterback was 13-8 as a starter with the Chiefs in 1992 and 1993?

12. Superstar tight end Tony Gonzalez wore what number jersey?

13. Which great Chiefs defensive lineman famously celebrated a sack by swinging an imaginary baseball bat?

14. True or false – The Chiefs have never picked a kicker or punter in the first round of the NFL Draft?

15. The longest interception return in franchise history was made by which defensive back against Seattle in December 1977?

16. What number jersey did star offensive lineman Will Shields wear?

17. True or false – Kicker Nick Lowery's given first name was Dominic?

18. Which Chiefs receiver, drafted in the third round in 2015, was born on an air force base in Turkey?

19.Chiefs wide receiver Elmo Wright was the first player in NFL history to do what? a) perform an end zone dance b) return three kicks for a touchdown in the same game c) fumble four times in a game

20. What is Derrick Johnson's middle name? a) Wayne b) Gordon c) O'Hara

Quiz 21: Answers

1. Hank Stram 2. Philadelphia 3. Todd Haley 4. Matt Nagy 5. Bob Sutton 6. Brett Veach 7. Marty Schottenheimer 8. Andy Heck 9. Haley 10. Hank Stram, Marty Schottenheimer and Andy Reid 11. True 12. Doug Pederson 13. Green Bay 14. Dick Vermeil 15. New York Jets 16. Bill Cowher 17. Minnesota 18. Arizona 19. a) 124 20. c) 13

Quiz 23: Numbers Game

Identify the jersey number that was worn by the following Chiefs players.

1. Alex Smith and Damon Huard

2. Travis Kelce and Tamarick Vanover

3. Trent Green and Pete Stoyanovich

4. Priest Holmes and Kevin Ross

5. Eric Berry and Albert Lewis

6. Kareem Hunt and Larry Johnson

7. Justin Houston and Mike Vrabel

8. Marcus Allen and Spencer Ware

9. Eric Fisher and Dave Lutz

10. Willie Lanier and Bill Maas

11. Deron Cherry and Benny Sapp

12. Dale Carter and Larry Johnson

13. Otis Taylor and Andre Rison

14. Rich Gannon and Albert Wilson

15. Marcus Peters and Dexter McCluster

16. Carlos Carson and Morris Stroud

17. Gary Green and Brandon Flowers

18. De'Anthony Thomas and Steve Bono

19. Nick Lowery and Morten Andersen

20. Dustin Colquitt and Kelly Goodburn

Quiz 22: Answers

1. Nick Lowery 2. Trent Green 3. Eric Berry 4. Justin Houston, Derrick Thomas, Jared Allen and Neil Smith 5. Manchester United 6. Tony Gonzalez 7. Running back 8. False 9. Will Shields 10. 12 times 11. Dave Krieg 12. #88 13. Neil Smith 14. True 15. Gary Barbaro 16. #68 17. True 18. Chris Conley 19. a) Perform an end zone dance 20. c) O'Hara

Quiz 24: Pot Luck

1. Which Chiefs running back won the Pro Football Weekly NFL Comeback Player of the Year award in 1990?

2. Chiefs linebacker Tamba Hali was born in which African country?

3. The Chiefs signed star running back Priest Holmes after he was released by which team?

4. Which elusive Chiefs return man was nicknamed 'The Human Joystick'?

5. French is the native language of which Chiefs offensive lineman who joined the team in 2014?

6. Which Chiefs receiver caught a pass in 83 straight games between 1985 and 1991?

7. What is the name of the trophy awarded to the winner of the AFC Championship game?

8. Which quarterback, best known for his time in Philadelphia, spent the final year of his pro career in 1989 in Kansas City?

9. True or false – The loudest crowd noise ever officially recorded was created by Chiefs fans at Arrowhead?

10. Who scored Kansas City's only rushing touchdown in Super Bowl IV?

11. Who scored Kansas City's only receiving touchdown in Super Bowl IV?

12. Which Kansas City defensive back went to the Pro Bowl every year from 1983 through to 1988?

13. Has Arrowhead ever hosted a Super Bowl?

14. Which linebacker did the Chiefs select with the 23rd overall pick in the 2014 NFL Draft?

15. Which Chiefs defensive back, who played with the team from 2008 through 2013, has the same name as the lead singer of the rock band The Killers?

16. True or false – When Arrowhead first opened was the playing surface made of grass or artificial turf?

17. The NFL Network's first ever live game was on Thanksgiving Day 2006 and featured the Chiefs against which division rival?

18. Which 2017 AFC West head coach spent 2 seasons with the Chiefs as a player in 1987 and 1988?

19. How many times did the Chiefs franchise win the AFL Championship? a) once b) twice c) three times

20. Worn by 24 different players between 1960 and 2016, what is the most issued jersey number in Chiefs history? a) 3 b) 24 c) 86

Quiz 23: Answers

1. #11 2. #87 3. #10 4. #31 5. #29 6. #27 7. #50 8. #32 9. #72 10. #63 11. #20 12. #34 13. #89 14. #12 15. #22 16. #88 17. #24 18. #13 19. #8 20. #2

Quiz 25: Anagrams

Rearrange the letters to make the name of a current or former Chiefs player or coach.

1. Exalts Him

2. End Diary

3. Save Tickler

4. Rent Regent

5. Make The Run

6. Mat Shrank

7. Snow Laden

8. Hostile Perms

9. Got Any Nozzle

10. New Bay Owed

11. Enlist Him

12. Market Orchids

13. Wonky Relic

14. Action Soars

15. Italy Roots

16. Scampers True

17. Nuclear Slam

18. Chief Riser

19. Wilier Foal

20. Maharajas Cell

Quiz 24: Answers

1. Barry Word 2. Liberia 3. Baltimore 4. Dante Hall 5. Laurent Duvernay-Tardif 6. Stephone Paige 7. Lamar Hunt Trophy 8. Ron Jaworski 9. True 10. Mike Garrett 11. Otis Taylor 12. Deron Cherry 13. No 14. Dee Ford 15. Brandon Flowers 16. Artificial turf 17. Denver 18. Jack Del Rio 19. c) Three times 20. c) 86

Made in the USA
Monee, IL
15 December 2019